Abecedarium

A Celebration of the Alphabet in Verse

by
Mark William Worthing

with art by
Morton Benning

© Mark Worthing 2019

All rights reserved. This book or any portion thereof may not be reproduced or used in any manner whatsoever without the express written permission of the publisher except for the use of brief quotations in a book review.

First Printing, 2019

ISBN 978-0-9924742-8-7

Cover and internal art by Morton Benning

Published in Australia by Immortalise via Ingram Spark

www.immortalise.com.au

Table of Contents

Poetic Preface..1
A, Aleph, Alpha...4
Bridesmaid B..6
Culture conscious C...8
Dynamic D..10
Enigma E...12
Feral F..14
Gallantly galumphing G..16
Heroic H..18
The dotted I..20
Judicious J...22
Kicking K..24
Liquid letter L...26
Middleman M..28
Eternal, unlimited N..30
Opulent O...32
Pro forma P...34
Queer, quirky Q...36
R never rests...38
Sensuous sibilant...40
T transfigured 42
U unfettered...44
Votive vox humana...46
Warp and waft of double U.......................................48
Exasperating X...50
De Y littera...52
Zed is not dead!...54
Notes on the Individual Stanzas...............................55

Poetic Preface

The alphabetisation of my childhood mind
occurred over long hours
in linoleum-tiled, chalk-filled
public school classrooms.
Ubiquitous were the rows of letters
running round the top
of pale brick walls.
In my head they danced,
fought and fumbled –
weaved their magic.
Some walked, others sat or ran.
Alternatingly fearsome and friendly,
each with its own personality manifest
in upper and lower case.
I spent years unlocking their secrets,
the variety of sounds represented by a single letter,
the strange effect they had
in combinations.
Their mysteries remained long
out of reach,
though eventually
they became my friends.

These poems pursue
the letters, twenty-six in all
of our English alphabet.
The unique personality of each,
seen in its form, friends, sounds.
Literary quotes and references,
alphabetic genealogies, alliterations,
religious allusions and alphabetic
psychoanalysis –
woven throughout.
In form and structure
the plan, simple:
twenty-six *vers libre* poems
twenty-six lines each.
Each poem linked,
chainlike,
from A to Z;
a poetic abecedarium,
celebrating a lifetime of wondering
at letters,
and four millennia of alphabetisation
of the human mind.

A, Aleph, Alpha

A, Aleph, Alpha
grown into runic Anglo oak;
ancient astrological ox,
horns turned down for headlong charge
through newly formed alphabet.
Or is it Victor Hugo's two friends shaking hands
in mid embrace – an alphabetic canopy.
Algebraic known quantity 'a'
or all-creating Alpha and Omega,
symbol of God's tripartite unity.
From beginning to end, we race,
laughing through Seuss's abecedary and
Aunt Annie's alligators asking Alice
whether Hester Prynne can ever forgive
the dark side of A,
begun for all in Adam's fall.
Meanwhile Andrew Aguecheek,
with no more wit than a Christian speaks:
'Abracadabra, open sesame.'
Big A, little a,
anaphoric key to childhood literacy –
literary celebrity:
Monarch Aleph, Jakob Grimm's king of vowels
and Hegel's pyramids,
or simply Wallace Steven's
infant A, standing on infant legs.

Bridesmaid B

Infant Gnostic Jesus
whom they bade pronounce Beth
rebuffed them with the meaning of Aleph.
Bridesmaid B
second place in Phoenician, Grecian,
Roman alphabets.
Belittled b,
indignity of B-grade teams and film.
Forehead branded B,
medieval blasphemy,
less interesting than branding sin of A.
But bold, beautiful B will not be denied;
it even boasts its own betabet
in ancient Gaelic Beth-luis-nion.
Blessed letter of Hebrew creation
bereshith bara
'In the beginning created God' B.
Be, bee, *Bienenstich*
tastes good with well-fed rotund letter B
while Ben bends Bim's broom
sweeping aside
unwanted building blocks to make room
for sacred letter B –
symbol of Urania,
better-known Miltonic muse
of poetry.

Culture conscious C

Poetry
of culture conscious consonantal C
awash in sea of unseen homophones.
Most unnecessary of letters
descended from Gimel and Gamma,
chameleon C encroaches
the phonetic confines
of k, s and q,
our mongrel androgynous C.
But comedian C collapses to ch,

inspired by Grecian, Cyrillic X
that Channing and Chaucer could scarce do without.
Caressing cursive C,
curvaceous, circular crescent
clothed in classic capitals.
Runic Cen and old Gaelic Coll
offspring of Calliope,
music muse of major scale
indispensable for science
with its Celsius calibrations,
measuring centigrade and centimetre,
carbon-chemistry C,
$E=MC^2$
and light speed c.
Unnecessary letter indeed.
Nothing is faster than C.

Dynamic D

Fast on the heels
of science dependent C,
dynamic D,
descendent of Daleth and Delta,
dances divinely
with Demeter, devil deity,
like Delilah delving into darkness
unbroken by runic Daeg.
In every self-respecting alphabet, D equals four.
Orwellian Boxer, who learned his letters up to D
dare not hope for more –
not from Noah Jacobs' altruistic
letter *par excellence*.
Defensive dental Ds pronounced
with tongue in cheek assent and gratitude.
Plato's Δ expressed binding rest in place,
and in higher maths big D and little d,
respectively,
stand for derivation and differentiation.
Dancing dingoes down-under play didgeridoos,
while Dogberry makes
much ado about nothing
and Dostoevsky and Odysseus,
with nothing better to do,
abbreviate Divus and Decius
to the distant drone of damning drums.

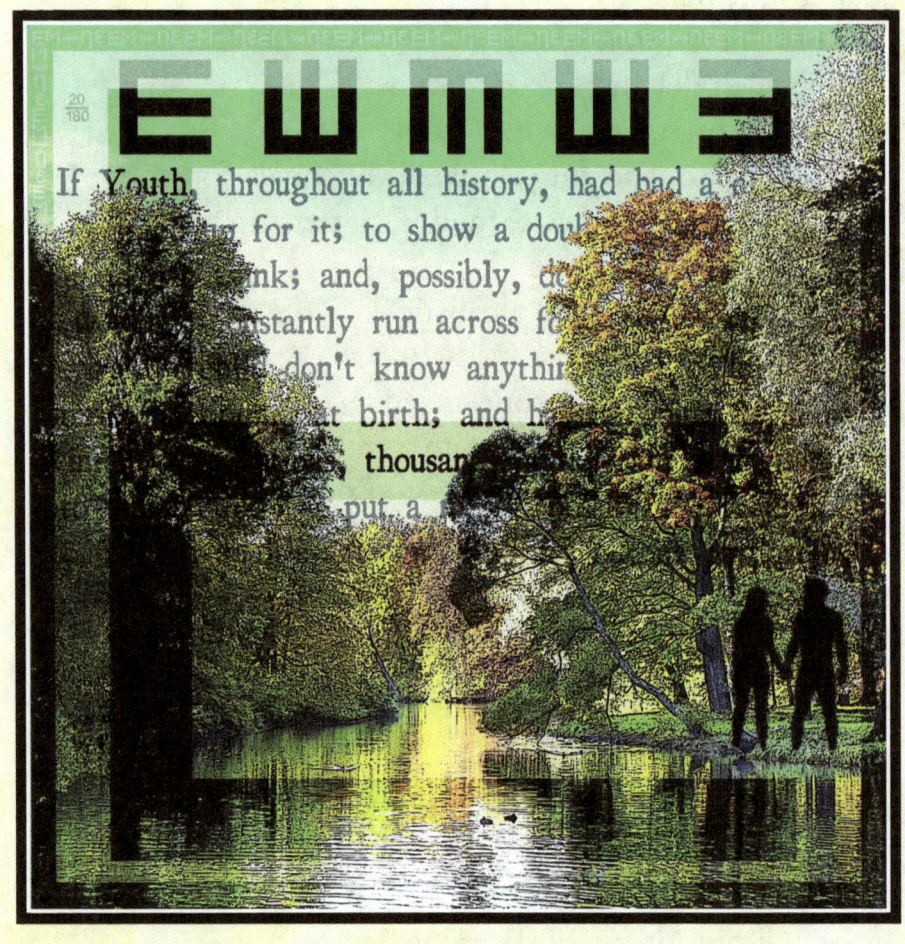

Enigma E

Distant Gaelic cousin Eadha
and runic equestrian Eh,
entwined with autumn equinox
cannot avoid
ever-present E –
most common English letter,
evolved from Hellenic Epsilon and Eta,
but evaded in E-allergic *Gadsby*.
ee cummings, of all people,
eschewed capital E, whereas in truth,
Victor Hugo found
foundation, pillar and roof;
each architectural element.
Eye test ∃E, end to end,
pointing up, down, left, right,
even East,
extending every direction from Eden
to Egypt, Eritrea and Ethiopia.
Enigma E,
E equals academic failure, yet
Einstein's E equals MC^2.
Even Eden's ever esteemed Eve
erred – emerged expelled,
clinging to one eternal
evocative vowel,
ever fallen, ever free.

Feral F

Free, fallen feral F,
big fat report card F –
a failure worse than E.
Ferocious FEE FI FO FUM,
angry friggin, fricken, F-off F,
bad boy of the alphabet.
Flimflam artists, fleecing felons.
Can any good fruit flow from F?
F, named in Greek Digamma
for two Gammas
fastened end to end
fell out of favour in that tongue.
Evil Dr Faustus used his letters
to facilitate foul formulas,
but our voiceless labiodental spirant
is by fortuned fate
not without some minor fanfare.
In runic, Feoh is first
and gave that alphabet the name, Futharc.
F, with far fewer credits than some,
found favour
with Fahrenheit, fluoride and fluorine.
F is freedom, fun,
frolics in full-sun
and possesses after all
full-fledged goodness despite its fall.

Gallantly galumphing G

Goodness, gracious
how Gimmel and Gamma have grown!
Semetic camel, born of Gemini
and Grecian Gamma
co-existed as C in Roman alphabet
'til Spurius Ruga,
circa 230 BC,
gave the voiced guttural stop
graciously, a tail,
guaranteeing G
gate seven, without fail.
Runic Gyfu, generous gift,
and Gaelic Gort, symbol of resurrection,
fill G with God-given goodness
marred only by the gammadion's
four fascist Gammas.
The genius of G, from Glogolitic to Gothic
has triumphed with gravity,
Gutenberg's movable type,
and Clio, muse of history;
not to mention Robert Louis Stevenson's
grade school vision of genie G
drinking from gilded goblet.
And so G goes galumphing
gallantly into the alphabet
with guttural gridiron grace.

Heroic H

H is gridiron goalposts
and lower case cushioned chair;
a breathing, unpronounced sound.
Did Siddharta ask,
'What is the sound of H?
Some say H is no sound or letter at all.
To remove her from the alphabet is their task.
But without breath there is no life.
Horatio, Hawthorne and Homer
wouldn't be the same
as Oratio, Awthorne and Omer.
And I've no need of air on my Ed.
What of hearth and home,
heroic Helloise
and bright shinning Helios,
Not to mention the fate
of hath, hither and hatch? –
a real H-horned dilemma.
But take heart, dear English H,
you may be only the sound of breathing
but by the host of heaven
we are herewith, hereby and henceforth hooked
on spiranted ch, ph, sh, and th,
and the voiced exhalation of Grecian Hermes
and Hellenic Herodotus,
father of history, and lies

The dotted I

Eyes, lies and more 'I's.
Irksome irony that
all-important I
should descend
from Semitic consonantal Yod
and Grecian Iota,
smallest letters of their alphabets.
Not one iota,
my four 'i'ed Mississippi,
shall be lost from 'I'.
Insisted Ambrose Bierce:
'I is the first word of the language,
the first thought of the mind,
the first object of affection' –
the I of the storm of me,
centre of a universe of 'I's,
in the shadow of I AM.
Iconographic Ichthus,
ingenious eye of faith and fish,
irreplaceable by I-Pod or I-Ching.
They are nothing without I-beam I, standing tall
and small i shyly blinking
at a gathering of Inklings.
and why must I,
I wondered once,
always dot my eyes?

Judicious J

A dot atop
a crooked i,
English J needs justify
its recent unacknowledged descent
from consonantal I,
and ousting joust with rival Y.
This queue-jumping decorative hook
has claimed its place at number 10,
our junior school umbrella J.
No proper letter some say.
What would Judge Judy do?
Rule judicious J a juvenile impostor I?
Jack and Jill,
prior to the incident on the hill,
join predictably the joint committee
legitimising J.
Apart from jail birds jaywalking
outside their alphabetic jurisdiction,
J brings jest, justice, joy –
and jukebox and jeans, fashion *de jour*.
Jingle, jangle, jiggling jelly,
jesters juggling jigs and juleps.
Could we lose belittled jokester J
To abecedary snobbery?
With Jesus' claim on jot and tittle
they dare not kick out J.

Kicking K

Kicking K,
kingly kaliph
descendent of Phoenician Kaph
and Grecian Kappa.
Double K and KKK
kabbalistic and Amerikan symbols of *kakon*/evil
loom over Kung Faux, katana and karate K,
perhaps still not quite OK
with its C-centred Eutruscan-Roman slight.
On any Kelvin scale, K
is the most combative letter of the alphabet.
Hence the silence of K,
like Shakespeare's tamed Katharina,
is out of place alike
in *k*nife and *k*night.
But our Kafkaesque letter comes to voice
with a kackling teutonic kikiri-ki,
for there is more to K
than Kid Kookaburra and Kelly Kangaroo
kidnapping Kitty Koala outside
Graeme's local K-Mart.
Indeed, Doc Kellog's leggy K
has boardroom clout with
kunnskaping karats, kilos and kwid.
So kudos to K –
a letter with heart.

Liquid letter L

Liquid letter L,
if Johnson shall be believed
'melteth in the sounding'
like its runic cousin Lagu
(or was that Lake Lago?);
and its lanky lower case earns
the laconic label
la lettre longue.
For Latin's L was the half century line
and number two for the denizens of Limerick
and their Gaelic Beth-luis-nion,
which our *literam longam* likes just fine
for L is no fighter like neighbour K
but languishing lover and
singer of luxuriant lullabies;
it is life and *libra* –
literate offspring of Lamed and Lambda
nourishing lettered literati
who read *Love's Labour Lost*
for the cost of a pizza and coke
and sometimes ponder why
Luke Luck likes lakes.
Lovely, legible L, lamppost of letters,
seldom lawless, lewd,
and never full of lies.
Lord help us, Amen.

Middleman M

A man in the middle,
symmetrical M,
mathematical centre of alphabet,
with classical capitals
and medieval mendicant minuscules.
Its mountainous twin peaks
are, *mutatis mutandis*, actually waves,
from pictographic Hebrew Mem.
Another liquid letter of easy virtue,
its bilabial nasal consonant
melting in the mouths
of small infants, calling 'Mama,'
the easiest of sounds,
in a myriad of cultures.
Mem is mystical sign for woman
while runic M stands for man,
and Gaelic Muin is simply the joy
of woman and man combined;
more *Roman*tic by a mile than M = 1,000.
And if the Dormouse and March Hare
want to draw everything beginning with M,
with much muchness of monkeys and mice,
Alice could not move
a more fitting monument
to our alphabetic
halfway mark.

Eternal, unlimited N

N is half an M,
or so that's the way
the voiced nasal consonant
always seemed,
nailed on the classroom wall.
While Nun and Nu are homophones
of Saxon now and new,
the negativity of N is hard to condone.
It gives us no, not, never, nor
nein, *nyet*, nil, nothing and more
nay – a full compliment of *nihil negativa*
negating a never-ending string of modifiers
with its non-stoppable non-
and unrelenting un-.
Who needs this Ash tree goblin
having manoeuvred its way to number three
in Beth-luis-nion tree alphabet?
Can nothing nice be said of N –
this *norma normans* of negation?
But N negates as well *das Nichtige*
renewing now the unrestrained
need to find an end to nothingness.
And so we glimpse double-negating
unending N, *nihil obstat* in hand,
extending to the Nth degree,
eternal, unlimited N.

Opulent O

'O King Eternal'
song of praise
omniscient, opulent O,
ancient symbol of eternity
and the One.
Sitting on top assonantal
oligarchy of vowels.
Once ultimate Omega
collapsed into Omicron's occupation
of mid-alphabet comfort,
transformed into monocled O,
descendent of Semitic Ayin.
Proto-pictogramic eye
looks on observing
Oscar's only ostrich
oiling an orange owl in Orrorroo.
But Seuss cannot reduce
the glory of O.
Tory's O triumphant,
Thurber's wonderful O
and Poe's most sonorous vowel.
Even Tolkien spent a year with OED
on over-looked, over-worked O.
Omega remains, beginning to end
a single divine circle
o' perfection.

Pro forma P

Perfect P,
a pie on porcelain pedestal.
Whether Pi, π, or P
the lip unvoiced stop presents
a plethora of etymological problems.
Hidden P of Psalm one-one-nine
proclaims authorship divine;
pops up on prefixes *pro forma*.
With its puddle paddle battle on a poodle
P presents problems aplenty
for phonetics, pronunciation, and
some kid named Peter
predestined to pine away
picking pecks of pickled peppers
and pernicious persimmons.
P, pizza and pretzel-eating party letter of the alphabet,
plays at pangrammatics and palindromes –
is poetics' most alliterated consonant.
Papyrus, parchments, paper,
formed of pulp beaten plants,
pressed for printed
prose portal plates on which P dances
with its twenty-five partners.
Plain old P possesses the transforming power
of Oz's properly pronounced Pyrzqxgl,
revealing the potency of P.

Queer, quirky Q

Potent queen
of guttural Ks,
descendent of Hebrew Qoph,
symbolised by the quince, of course,
in Gaelic Beth-luis-nion.
Yet like Quirinius, governs
under a question.
Queer, quirky Q with squiggly tail
queues up quietly before
consonantal U.
Ben Jonson would have her abdicate
her losing battle with K
in Qabbala, Quran and Qibla.
Q, lone letter that cannot
quit a word.
But quiet now, for the quick Queen of Quincy,
proclaims Q is quickened, not dead.
Who would ever mind a P without a Q,
or imagine James Bond or barbie without Q –
What quintessential quackery!
Q is quilted into our every quote and query
the I.Q. of Quincy Adams
is quite unnecessary
to ask the question:
What would U do
without Q?

R never rests

Without remorse
R rolls off Germanic tongues
with a rhythm and pace befitting
the only letter that runs,
like some rugged rascal,
round the ragged rocks;
R never rests.
From Phoenician Resh to Grecian Rho,
rampant, racing R,
Rolls-Royce of letters, relishes
the role assigned by Socrates as the letter of motion.
But for the poet Persius, R is
the *litera canina*,
that snarling, growling canine letter.
Rolling, running, growling R
requites its reputation for action, yet
remains remarkably renown
in the realm of rhotics,
for reading, 'riting and 'rithmetic –
and religion, replete with revered repertoire of
revival, ritual and resurrection.
A restive renaissance letter
whose rhetoric is rich in
rhyme and rhythm,
and like runic cousin Rad,
rarely simply riding.

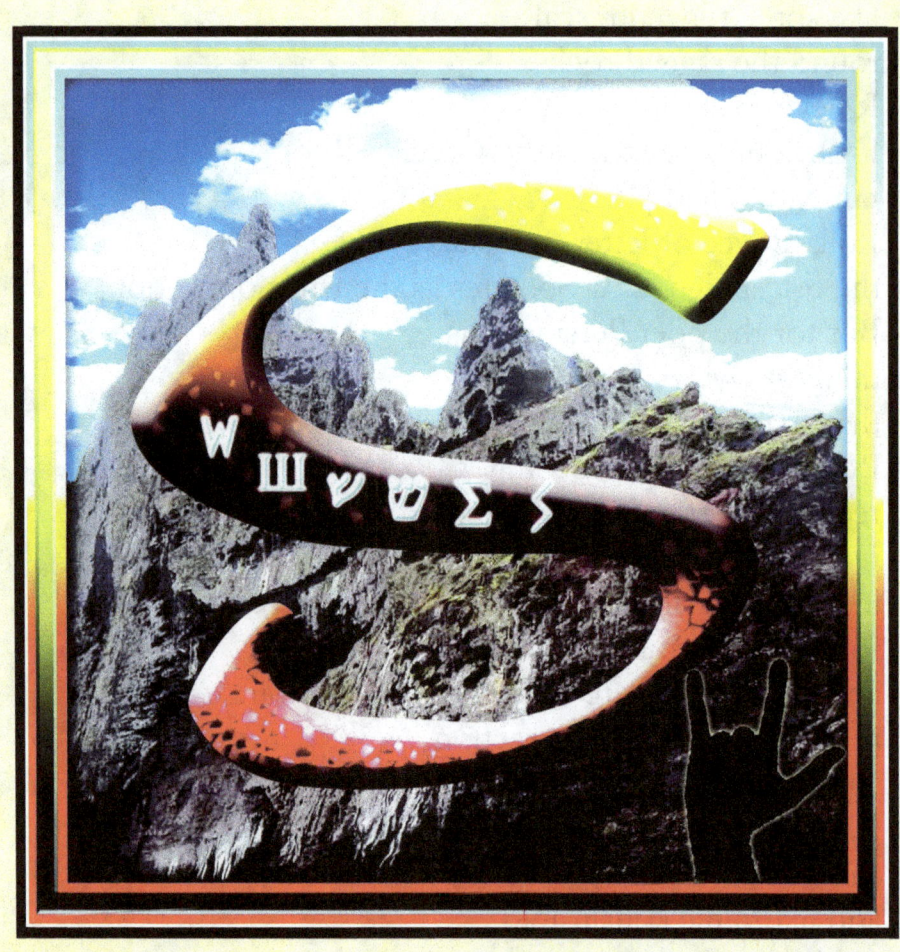

Sensuous sibilant

This simple sibilant
suffers surely some
form of schizophrenia;
simul justus et peccator,
at the same time saint and sinner.
As Semetic Shin she was the
Shabbat shalom,
sacred descendent of Proto-Sinaitic,
alphabeticus originalis;
and later, Latin *spiritus sanctus*,
saintly from sacrament to sermon.
But her slithering serpentine form suggests
something more sinister than Sally
selling seashells by the seashore.
The selfish, shifty, seedy side of S spells
scandal and shame with
seditious schemes
and succubus seduction enshrining a scion of shadow
into our letter, *sans serif*.
For sin without S
is a mere shrivelled preposition.
So beware the scarlet S
and speak *shibboleth* succinctly
or suffer the consequences
before Justice Shallow
of this tumultuous sibilant.

T transfigured

Tumultuous T,
twentieth letter,
thunderous and triumphant,
testifies, at the turning-point of literacy,
to texts, tablets, tongues, translations,
standing tall at the tail of
Hebrew and pre-Homeric alphabets.
But T was always touted for
theistic transposition.
Thane of Theos, its divine transmission
is told in Plato's tale of Theuth,
whose alphabet the tyrant Thamus
typically – turned down.
Then other Titans, Thalia, comedic muse,
and Thor, god of thunder
staked title to T.
Yet T, most religious of letters
for two thousand years
testified in cruci-form as Grecian Tau
to the Christian
tree of life and death
upon which the Christ,
tortured and transformed,
transfigured into talismanic T,
transfixing us
with transcendental truth.

U unfettered

The truth of U
lies in its ubiquitous, uncial smile.
Separated from its umbilical, consonantal sibling V
under Renaissance duress
from Ulysses' ancestral Upsilon,
U now stands unbound, unique.
Upside down umbrella U,
fifth of vowels,
sung in unison by
unlettered urchins and
Goethe's chanting demons alike;
'Aa! Ee! I! O! U!
What is that to you!'
Unlike More's unused Utopian alphabet,
the utility of U is
ultimately undisputed –
its power lying uncannily,
in its unmatched ability
to unburden untold adjectives
of unbidden, unwanted meaning.
Unflinching companion of Q and
un-disputed, under-rated, uni-vocal, ultra-mundane,
Über-menschlich, Ur-geschichtlich,
up-start queen of prefixes;
U is unmistakably
unfettered.

Votive vox humana

Unfettered from vexatious work of vowels
this pointy variant of U
has vanquished its variform vassal
after veritable centuries of vexation
between the urn and vase,
as Victor Hugo volunteered.
V is now free to voice
its votive *vox humana*
in thanks for its own volition.
Yet versatile V vacillates
vice versa
from victor to victim.
It is the vincible letter of the vulgar
of vermin and vermiculture
and the *Biblia Vulgata*,
villain of versions.
But V is mostly valued for victorious valour,
and Victor V. Vulture
vexatiously vocalising
V's verdant victories,
vigorous verbiage,
and veritable vortex of verse
vindicating its virtues.
V has our vote
this *voix céleste* of vespers
no longer doubling as a vowel.

Warp and waft of double U

This double V
named oddly double U,
weird offspring of the war
waged twixt alphabetic predecessors.
Unknown to Greco-Romans,
and by close Germanic kin, poorly spoken,
W is Anglo-Saxon's contribution
to the world of written sound,
wending its way warily from Celtic Wyn.
Why would English need its own letter?
Need we ask? What would we do
without Why? What? Where? When?
Not to mention Whither? Whence? and Whereupon?
Our speech would lose its warp and waft
and poor Walt Whitman, what a loss!
My childhood 'winter, water, wonderland'
laid waste for want of
wicked warrior WASPs
asking after the whereabouts of Wally.
Whatever the work,
whether welfare or weather,
no words wear so well
nor wield the same weight
in our whimsical English *Wortschatz*
than those upon which W stands
at the font.

Exasperating X

From font of X
spring few true words
Xylophone, Xenophobe, Xerox ... and we are done.
Even Graeme Base
illustrator extraordinaire,
cheated on X with smoke and mirrors!
Though X as a symbol,
like lookalike Grecian Chi,
has proven useful in extreme
with X-box, x-ray, x-rated, x-factor
XXXX beer, X marks the spot
and that all important x-chromosome.
Still, one wonders why Wallace Stevens spoke
of 'vital, arrogant, fatal, dominant X.'
Of noted names X yields but three:
Saintly Xavier, royal Xerxes and authorial Xenophon.
Of famous places only two:
Xanthus, which no longer exits,
And Xanadu, which never did.
As for deities but one: Xipe, Aztec god of planting.
And in mythology Xanthus again,
half a team of Achilles' immortal horses.
Alas there are no more.
For X, exasperating –
nonetheless,
X comes in at number XXIV.

De Y littera

Y is letter XXV
and there some say,
we should have stayed,
with youthful yaks yodelling
the virtues of yurts and yetis
in Yoda-speak
from Ypsilon Y stems, it does.
From ages yore it's been the letter
of philosophy and destiny
invented by Pythagoras,
even the letter of tetragrammatonic personal divinity.
Youthful students of the yeshiva yammer;
yadda, yadda, yadda.
Y is the shape of moral choice,
a fork in the road; that which must be.
Why is Hercules caught between Pleasure and Virtue?
Were yin and yang unknown in yesteryear?
Y is the first letter to inspire a poem.
Maximinus yielded twelve stanzas
in 'De Y littera,'
retelling the Samian yarn of herculean yearning.
Yea more could be said, if not for the yawns,
of yorkers and yo-yos;
yogis, yobbos, yuppies
and yes,
even Yanks.

Zed is not dead!

Yankee Zee,
everywhere to see.
But Zed is not dead,
thank you very much,
Quenton Tarantino
and pseudonymous zealot Shakespeare
who cried with *zeitgeistlich* zest:
'Thou whoreson Zed!
Thou unnecessary letter!'
Zounds! What a zinger!
Proud descendant of Zeta and Zayin
banished from Rome
by the censor Claudius Caecus,
circa 312 BC,
before zipping back to find its place
at alphabet's end
in this zany zero-sum game.
While Z has now the distinction of two names,
it's zigzag history through English,
from zilch to zenith, saw it variously labelled
Izzard, Uzzard, Ezod, Zard and Zad –
a ziggurat of appellatives
for zesty Zed and Zeppelins –
gadzooks – a zeugma! –
zymotic abecedarian outgrowth of
A, Aleph, Alpha.

Notes on the Individual Stanzas

Oddly, many early readers of the poem found some of the allusions obscure. So, bowing to pressure, I have put together this appendix, far longer than the poem itself, as an explanation of the many literary, historical, religious, phonetic, cultural, foreign language and alphabetic allusions in the poem. But before reading the following explanations, try to work out as many of the references and allusions as possible.

The astute observer will also notice that many of the poetic references have been incorporated into the illustrations. For puzzle solvers with a bit of OCD, Morton Benning has also included, often hidden, the number represented by each letter within the illustration. These are only rarely in the form of Arabic numerals, so you will have to look closely to find them all.

Aleph and Alpha are, respectively, the Hebrew and Greek ancestors of A. Another of their alphabetic descendants was the runic symbol for the vowel sound A in the so-called tree alphabet used in pre-Anglo Britain. The tree character for this sound was the oak. Phoenician Aleph (a close predecessor to the Hebrew) meant ox and was connected to the star sign Taurus. Indeed Phoenician and early Hebrew versions of Aleph looked like our capital A laid on its side, or an ox head with its horns pointing out, ready to charge. One of the more poignant images of A is that of French dramatist and poet Victor Hugo (1802-1885), who saw in the letter the image of two friends shaking hands while leaning in to embrace one another. Clearly he was someone who spent a lot of time in primary school starring at these strangely fascinating symbols, letting his imagination run with the images.

In algebra 'a' is one of the most common symbols and represents some known quantity. The connection of the letter to the divine comes chiefly in two forms: the title 'Alpha and Omega' (the Greek equivalent of A and Z) as an appellation of God, and the use of A as a medieval symbol of the trinity owing to its three sides and three points all forming a single letter. A as beginning of the alphabet is often associated with the end. A is the start which leads us 'racing' through the entire alphabet, often learned with the aid of children's abecedaries. One of the most famous of these abecedaries in recent times is that produced by Theodor S. Geisel, a.k.a. 'Dr Seuss' (1904-1991) in 1963 who began with the question 'Big A little a what begins with a?' And the answer learned by so many of my generation was of course, 'Aunt Annie's alligator,' which made no sense at all but was wonderfully alliterative and visual. Alice is a reference to Alice Liddell, daughter of the well-known Professor of Classical Greek, H. G. Liddell of Cambridge University (of Liddell-Scott Greek lexicon fame), and inspiration to Charles Dodgson, a.k.a. Lewis Carroll (1832-1898).

But A is not all light and fun and children's games. It also recalls the character Hester Prynne from Nathaniel Hawthorne's (1804-1864) *The Scarlet Letter* who was forced to wear a red letter A on her dress when she was found guilty of adultery in Puritan New England. The use of scarlet letters to brand adulterers was a real and relatively recent memory for Hawthorne who was born at Salem, Massachusetts and was descended from one of the judges of the Salem witchcraft trials. 'Begun for all in Adam's Fall' is a reference to the famous beginning of the abecedary in *The New England Primer* of 1687 which teaches A with 'In Adam's Fall, we sinned all' and appears about the same general time as the setting for Hawthorne's novel. Shakespeare, who was more than a little sceptical of the emerging Puritan theology and the church in general, created the character Andrew Aguecheek in *Twelfth Night* whose most famous line is: 'Methinks sometimes I have no more wit than a Christian.' At the time 'wit' was commonly used to express a biting and clever sense of humour, for which the church was not known.

'Abracadabra' is simply a fun word with a lot of 'a's. Its origins are cabalistic and it was written in triangular form, like capital A. But the word also evokes the idea of a magic spell and the opening up of secrets, which A does as the start of the alphabet, unlocking the mysteries of literacy through its repetition, similar to the repetition of key words as a rhetorical device, which is known as anaphora. A is thus the key to our learning literacy as children. This makes A a very real literary celebrity honoured by many literary greats. Jakob Grimm (1785-1863), the eldest of the two Grimm brothers, held A to be king of the vowels. The German philosopher Georg Wilhelm Friedrich Hegel (1770-1831) thought of pyramids when he saw the letter. And American modernist poet Wallace Stevens (1879-1955) described A in stanza two of his poem, 'An Ordinary Evening in New Haven,' as 'infant A, standing on infant legs' as a more apt image of reality than 'twisted, stooping, polymathic Z.'

Speaking of infants, the infancy narratives in the second-century Gnostic Gospel of St Thomas, which purports to tell stories of what the child Jesus was like with all his divine powers, gives the account of his teacher asking him to pronounce 'Beth,' the second letter of the Hebrew and Aramaic alphabet, and the predecessor of our B. It was a logical pedagogical progression, but the young Jesus refused to move on through his lessons in the alphabet unless his teacher could first tell him the meaning of Aleph (or A) The child Jesus went through two teachers in this way, withering the arm of one who dared smack him, and striking the other dead. After this, Jesus' parents had no choice but to home school him! It was the beginning of B's troubles.

Poor B – always the bridesmaid. It has held second spot in all the significant predecessor alphabets to our own, and because of this, anything that is second rank is always B-grade. Like A, it even had its own branding sin and was burned into the foreheads in medieval England of those found guilty of blasphemy – but even in this, it was a much less interesting and spectacular sin than adultery. Poor B couldn't seem to get a break in its battle with A.

But B did have it victories and claims to fame. In the ancient Gaelic alphabet, known after its first three letters as Beth-luis-nion, it came first, and was the symbolic equivalent of A. Also, the first two words of the Hebrew and Christian scriptures, from Genesis 1:1, are *bereshith bara* (literally "In the beginning created ..."

Most South Australians know and love *bienenstich*, a popular Barossa Valley dessert which, in German, literally means 'Bee sting,' though interestingly there seems to be no dessert by this name in Germany. Of course, this reminds us that B is perhaps our chubbiest letter, and does seem to enjoy its desserts.

'Ben bends Bim's broom' is taken from *Fox in Socks*, by Dr Seuss (Theodor Seuss Geisel 1904-1991) and is part of a story about Ben and Bim and their brooms which contains at one point 34 successive words beginning with B, spread through eleven sentences, and concludes with 'My poor mouth can't say that. No, sir. My poor mouth is much too slow, sir.' And while thinking of B and childhood one cannot resist the reference to building blocks. Finally, B also had a sacred connection in Greek mythology where it was the symbol of Urania, the muse of astronomy. The muses were the nine daughters of Zeus and Mnemosyne and each was assigned a department of art, literature or science to preside over and each had a letter symbol. Urania became a poetic muse to John Milton (1608-1674), who wrote in book seven of *Paradise Lost*: 'Descend from heaven, Urania, by that name if rightly thou art called, whose voice divine following above the Olympian hill I soar …' Indeed, during the Renaissance she began to be generally considered the muse of Christian poets, who were concerned with 'heavenly' things.

If Urania is the muse of Renaissance poets, she must have favoured C, for it is one of the most used and alliterated letters in poetry. It is a consonant conscious of its culture and class. Yet it is also awash in a sea of homophones, that is, words that sound the same but have different spellings, precisely because it has such a phonetic overlap with the letters K, S and Q. Even though it has a good pedigree, descending from Hebrew Gimmel and Greek Gamma, both also the third letters of their alphabets, it has abandoned their sound to English G and drifted into the territory of others. It has been called an unnecessary letter because the sounds it represents can all be equally well represented by K, S, and Q, thus making it in its present form and position something of a mongrel. So from the beginning, our elegant, cultured, classy C has a fight on its hands to justify its existence.

The reference to Comedian C is an allusion to Wallace Stevens' (American poet, 1879-1955) poem 'The Comedian as the letter C,' which he wrote because he felt all the shades of sound that C has adapted have a comic aspect to them. C as comedian has the last laugh and is not without an apologetic. Its defence begins with its use with H to form 'ch' sounds, which in Greek and its offspring Cyrillic (Russian and Slavonic) were formed with a X (Chi). But that symbol has taken up other duties in our alphabet. Sh makes another sound altogether, and kh and qh simply don't work. Channing and Chaucer are two English language writers from two different countries and two very different times. Their names depend on the availability of a C to join to an H and remind us of the importance of C to literature. They also happen to be the middle names of my two oldest sons.

The next part of C's defence has simply to do with its beauty. It is smooth and curvaceous, a perfect geometric crescent, with decorative ends when clothed in the form of classical capitals. In runic it was called Cen, and in Gaelic it was known as Coll, which reminds us of Calliope, one of the nine daughters of Zeus and Mnemosyne and was the muse of music. In whatever form, it is a beautiful letter and its sounds are associated with beauty.

For the third and final part of our defence of C we turn to science, which could scarce do without the letter. The entire metric system is reliant on centimetres, centigrams, and centigrades, not to mention the Celsius scale. C is also central to the world's most famous equation, Einstein's $E=MC^2$ which says that in any given system, such as the universe, the total energy (E) equals the total mass (M) times the speed of light (C) squared. C is the universal symbol for the speed of light, 300,000 kilometres per second. It has long been an axiom of science that nothing can travel faster than the speed of light, a.k.a. C.

D is another letter with a very ancient pedigree and is a direct descendant of Hebrew and Phoenician Daleth and Greek Delta. In Greek it is the first letter of Demeter (literally earth mother), goddess of the harvest, but also the presider over the cycle of life and death. Her grief at the imprisonment of her daughter Persephone by Hades in the Underworld is the cause of the six months of winter. In Hebrew Daleth is the first letter in the name of Delilah, who deceived her lover Samson (Judges 16). So there is a tinge of darkness to this letter.

Significantly, it is the fourth letter of the alphabet in Hebrew, Greek and English and is often used to symbolise the number four. Having stopped at D, four is also the number of letters learned by George Orwell's Boxer, a hard working cart horse in *Animal Farm* (1945) who is meant to symbolise the Russian working class.

Noah Jacobs, a delightful commentator on language and author of *Naming Day in Eden* and *The Toils of Language* considered D altruistic because of all that it has given. For the philosopher Plato, the letter Delta, with its firm base, illustrated a solid binding to its place. And mathematicians, too, have found use for the letter, with capital D standing for derivation, and small d standing for differentiation. For a bit of alliterative fun, we have the very Australian line, 'dancing dingos down-under play didgeridoos.' While in more serious literature there is Shakespeare's character Dogberry from *Much Ado about Nothing*, with his memorable line, 'O that I had been writ down an ass!' On the theme of literature we remember the great nineteenth-century Russian writer Fyodor Dostoevsky (1821-1881) and Homer's (8th century BCE) heroic Odysseus from his Epic poem *The Odyssey*.

Divus is a Latin adjective denoting deity. When Caesar Augustus, of Christmas play fame, died in Rome in 14 CE, the Senate famously declared him *divus*, that is, the deified one who was to be worshipped. Ironically, while Jesus was born under his reign, Augustus' deification by the Senate and the failure in the coming centuries of Jesus' followers to recognise this divinity, cost many their lives, especially under the reign of Gaius Messius Quintus Decius (249-251), who instituted the first empire-wide persecution of Christians. Damning distant drums indeed.

E, which has sister letters in the Gaelic and Runic alphabets, is the most common letter in English. Like the equinoxes, it cannot be avoided. Though this did not prevent novelist Ernest Vincent Wright from trying. In 1939, as the world was rushing to war, he wrote a 50,000

word novel about a dying city called Branton Hills, with a main character called John Gadsby (not to be confused with the much more famous and similarly named Gatsby from F. Scott Fitzgerald.) The memorable point from Wright's novel – and according to critics of the time it certainly wasn't the plot – was that he wrote the entire thing without using the letter 'e'. Not all agreed that 'e' could be so easily dispensed with, though poet e.e. cummings (1894-1962) did refuse to capitalise it. Victor Hugo saw in the letter a lesson in complete architecture, writing in *Voyages and Excursions* (1910): 'E is the foundation, the pillar and the roof – all architecture contained in a single letter.'

The letter in its capital form also evokes images of eye tests, which makes one think of directions, one of which is East, which in turn recalls the famous line from Genesis 'east of Eden,' (also the title of a novel by some fellow called Steinbeck, 1902-1968) which leads one to consider the theories that Eden was in Africa, which leads us to think of famous lands in Africa that begin with the letter E. Which all goes to show what can happen when the mind is allowed to drift freely with the letter E!

E also has a scientific connection, beginning with enigma, which can be a mystery to solve, or a code for Alan Turing (1912-1954) and company to break. But most famously in the world of science, E is one whole side of Einstein's famous equation.

But, back to Eden (science can be too dull) we think of Eve, one of its most famous residents. If E can equate to academic failure, it also symbolised Eve and Adam's moral failure with words like 'err' and 'expelled.' Yet even fallen, they were not without hope, for the Fall itself is a result of freedom, and from this an entire theology of freedom, sin and redemption might be constructed under the inspiration of this one evocative vowel.

If E introduces us to the Fall, F takes us all the way through it. It is truly a letter with a very bad reputation. F is the one letter dreaded even more than E on school report cards. No one, especially not one having stolen golden egg laying geese, likes to hear the warning roar: FEE FI FO FUM (from the English fairy tale, 'Jack and the Beanstalk'), and F has become so synonymous with a certain swear words in English that we need not spell out the word or words intended, the letter F by itself will do. And if not, we use 'replacement' words such as fricken and friggin. Then, of course, one thinks of many other negative words beginning with F such as flimflam, fleeced, felon, fruit fly, etc. Clearly, it will take some effort to redeem the reputation of the letter F.

The shape of our letter came from the Greeks, who called it a Digamma (literally two Gammas) when two Gammas were fastened end to end. But they never really found much use for it and it was largely forgotten. When literature picked it up with Dr Faustus, we found him only using it for foul formulas, so not much help here for a letter that phoneticists tell us is simply what we use to designate a voiceless labiodental spirant.

But when looking deeper we discover that in Runic the letter Feoh is listed first, and gave the name Futharc to that ancient alphabet. F also gets a bit of a positive run in science, with fluoride, fluorine and Fahrenheit, which is the unit of measuring heat still used in the US. And, despite the Fall, which is always capitalised to make a point, it is not hard to think of many words beginning with F that have positive connotations, such fun, favour and freedom.

The letter G has its origins in Hebrew Gimmel and Greek Gamma. Interestingly, in the Phoenician alphabet, from which Hebrew is descended, it is thought the letter Gimmel originally arose from a pictogram of a camel. The G sound, a voiced guttural stop, was covered by C in the old Latin alphabet until about 230 BCE when, according to Plutarch, Spurius Carvilus Ruga, the freed slave of the Roman Consul Spurius Maximus Ruga, and founder of the world's first private primary school, brought an end to the confusion between the two distinct sounds covered by C and placed the new G with its tail in the seventh place in his school's alphabet. So while the G sound existed in other alphabets, the form of our English letter has come from Ruga's not so 'spurious' innovation.

In some other alphabets the letter representing the G sound had significant symbolism. In the Runic alphabet one of its two letters signifying a G sound, Gyfu, means generous gift (the other, 'ger', meant year). And in Gaelic, the letter Gort is a symbol of resurrection. This positive imagery, however, is somewhat undone by the so-called gammadion, which is four capital Greek Gammas laid head to head, forming a swastika, though this was originally meant as a symbol of well-being in ancient Greece, and was also an early version of the Christian cross.

The letter G has significance in the history of languages and alphabets with not only Gaelic starting with a G sound, but also Gothic, now known primarily as a type of old German script, and Glogolitic, which is the name of the alphabet used in old 'Church Slavonic.' Then, of course, there is the famous invention of Johannes Gutenberg from 1452 of the printing press, who would have been personally thankful for the existence of the letter G.

On a more playful note, Robert Louis Stevenson (1850-1894), another young lad who liked to spend time looking at letters dreaming about their sacred lives, envisioned G when he was a child as a genie drinking from a goblet. It is also not hard to visualise G galumphing, a word made up by Lewis Carroll (a.k.a. Charles Lutwidge Dodgson, 1832-1898) for his poem 'Jabberwocky', which most take to be a somewhat less graceful and perhaps more enthusiastic and gallant version of galloping. I think of G charging forward through the alphabet like a helmeted knight, which conjures the image of American Gridiron players, whose helmets look remarkably like a capital G.

The link between G and H is clear, with gridiron helmeted G kicking a goal through the upright H that stands at either end of an American football field. Though, for many school children, 'h' in its lower case form looked like a cushioned chair upon which they could sit while learning their letters. Because H is a breathing, unpronounced sound, it sometimes seems to lack real substance, existing largely to show the effect it has on the following vowel. Hence the quip about Siddharta asking about the sound of

H which is a play not only on the breathing H of Siddharta Buddha, but also the famous question from his Zen followers centuries later about the sound of one hand clapping. Some have argued H isn't a real letter. But imagine an alphabet without the breathing sound of H – hence the saying, without breath, there is no life.

Imagine famous literary names like Horatio (a character in Shakespeare), Nathaniel Hawthorne, or the famous Greek poet Homer without the H. Many common words like hair, head and hearth would become other words entirely without the breathing sound of H. And imagine the fates of hath, hither and hatch, or of the many spiranted sounds like ch, ph, sh and th created with the aid of H. In all, the letter H would seem safe, from the time of the Greek god Hermes, messenger of the gods, and the Athenian writer Herodotus (484-425 BCE), who has the dubious distinction of being known as both the father of history and of lies, the later attribute given by those who did not agree with his history!

From the lies of history we move to eyes and I's. I is an important and busy letter, but its pedigree from Greek and Hebrew is the smallest and most inconsequential. Hence Jesus' famous saying that not a single jot (Hebrew letter Yodh) or tittle (Hebrew *keraia* – a line ending or serif) should pass away from God's written word. Or in more modern idiom we speak of 'one iota.' In American classrooms the letter I was famous for its starring role in the name Mississippi, which children all learned to spell as M-I-double S-I-double S-I-double P-I. Any child missing one of Mississippi's four 'I's knew they were well off the mark.

I is also one of two, or possibly three letters (if we count O rather than 'Oh') which form a word on its own. And what a word this is. I is the beginning of so many of our thoughts and sentences. Some call it the first word of the language because we learn quickly to say 'I want …' The well-known quote from Ambrose Bierce's *The Devil's Dictionary* (1911) begins: 'I is the first letter of the alphabet, the first word of the language.'

And I, too, has its strong religious connections. God's name as revealed in the Pentateuch was simply 'I AM,' and early Christians used the letters of the Greek word for fish (Ichthus/ἰχθύς) as an anagram for Jesus Christ, God's Son, Saviour (Ἰησοῦς Χριστὸς Θεοῦ Υἱὸς Σωτήρ). We also begin a number of words simply with I, such as I-Pod and I-Ching, and more significantly, I-beam, so called because that is the exact shape of the thing. And going back to eyes, lower-case 'i' does look like an eye blinking. And blinking rhymes with Inklings, the name of the famous writers group that included J.R.R. Tolkien, C.S. Lewis and Charles Williams, all of whom had I in their family name. A mere coincidence? Perhaps. But have you ever as a child wondered why you were told to always dot your eyes?

Only J, which follows I, also requires a dot. In many ways, it is simply a crooked little 'i'. The reason, of course, is that it is in fact a glorified I elevated to consonantal status. Only English has a J that is not only a letter but also a distinctive consonantal sound. Other languages use either I or Y for this task, or at least for what approximates the sound. Yosef instead of Joseph, for instance. Uniquely English J has found a place in the alphabet at number 10, a fitting address (thinking of No. 10 Downing Street) for a letter so strongly connected to all issues juridical. But still, the whimsical image of J with its umbrella, of Jack and Jill and jaywalking, J has always struggled to be taken seriously as something greater than an English innovation.

It is a whimsical and fun letter, giving us 'jingle jangle' from Gene Autry's country music hit of 1962, and 'jigs and julips' from the title of Virginia Cary Hudson's delightful *O Ye Jigs and Juleps*, published the same year. But as our unique letter of the alphabet, we English speakers are proud of our letter J and will defend it against all alphabetic snobbery. After all, Jesus begins with the letter and sound of J – or is that only in English?

K is a letter with more than a little kick. Its ancestors are Phoenician and Hebrew Kaph and Greek Kappa. The Etruscans and Romans used a hard C instead of a K, so the English alphabet went back to the earlier languages to pick up K as distinct from C, which was now mostly soft. Kaliph is an alternate spelling of caliph, which is similar in meaning to king in Arabic. The letter's martial connotations stem from kicking, killing, Kung-Fu, katana (the Japanese Samurai long sword) and karate, with the more silent knife and knight reinforcing its image. And by the way, Kung-Faux is fake Kung Fu fighting, as seen in movies.

But K it is also tainted with *kakon*, Greek for 'evil' and the cabalistic (also earlier kabalistic) symbol of misfortune and malice. Double K is a reference to an old cabalistic symbol of evil. The great humanist scholar Desiderius Erasmus alluded to this when he said that KK 'signifies two evil things opposed to a good one.' Nor can K escape the awful symbolism of the Klu Klux Klan (KKK).

But it is not all bad for K. In Shakespeare the tamed 'shrew' was named Katharina, and in science K represents Kelvin, a unit for the measurement of heat. Among writers Kafka is perhaps our most famous K, and in his native German, the rooster says kikiri-ki, instead of cock-a-doodle-doo, though one wonders how the rooster knows in which language to crow. Australian fauna also have a fondness for the letter. In Graeme Base's *Animalia* it is outside a K-Mart that Kid Kookaburra and Kelly Kangaroo kidnap Kitty Koala.

And we attribute K importance with kilos, karats, and kwid (a thousand units of the standard currency of your choice). We even have the Norwegian *kunnskaping*, which has crept into English, and means creating intellectual capital. K is indeed special, and not only for Dr Kellog.

Samuel Johnson (1709-1784) said L melted in the sounding of the letter. In Runic the sound is represented by Lagu, which sounds like Lago (Italian for lake). The French called lower case 'l' the long letter, and the Romans used it numerically to represent the number 50. For Gaelic speakers (which included those in the Irish town of Limerick) the letter Luis was second in their alphabet and was used to represent the number two. Libra is not only a horoscope sign, but the Latin word for scales. Because it was a unit of weight, it was the basis for pound, which is still abbreviated 'lb', short for libra.

The letter L is descendent from Hebrew Lamed and Greek Lambda. Shakespeare had a bit of a play with alliterating L in the title *Love's Labour's Lost*. And Literati is the name of the writing group I belong to, which for many years (before we became health conscious) used to meet over pizza and coke. 'Luke Luck likes lakes' is a tongue twister from Dr Seuss's *Fox in Socks* for those who struggle with the L sound. And L also looks like a lamppost and is sometimes illustrated as such in children's alphabets.

M is a symmetrical letter that appears (together with N) at the centre of the English alphabet. Mendicant (begging) monks would have written the letter often in medieval manuscripts as a minuscule. It looks like twin mountain peaks, but probably comes from a pictographic image of waves from the Hebrew Mem. Whether waves, or twin mountain peaks, the comparison is made, *mutatis mutandis*, which is a Latin phrase used when comparing two or more things or situations, in this case waves and mountain peaks. The term literally means 'the necessary changes having been made.' The sense is that even though there are changes to be made, or differences between the two things being compared, the basic point remains the same.

As a bilabial nasal consonant it is easy to pronounce and one of the first sounds infants can easily make. Hence ma, mama, mummy, omi, etc. Perhaps this is also why Hebrew Mem is the mystical sign for woman. Yet Runic M represents man, and Gaelic Muin represents woman and man coming together, which is far more interesting than M representing 1,000 in Latin.

In *Alice's Adventures in Wonderland*, Lewis Carroll has the Dormouse explain to Alice that the March Hare and the Mad Hatter were in the well 'drawing' everything that began with the letter M 'such as mouse-traps, and the moon, and memory, and muchness – you know you say things are "much of a muchness" – did you ever see such a thing as a drawing of a muchness?' And monkeys and mice is a vague allusion to Steinbeck's *Of Mice and Men*, in which another primate has been substituted.

If M is half-way through the alphabet, then it is fitting that the second half begins with half an M. Hebrew Nun and Greek Nu are pronounced the same as German *nun* (now) and English new. But the positives seem to end here with a lot of negativity associated with N. Most languages use an N-word for their basic word of negation. And the allusion to *nihil negativa* (lit. the nothing of negation) is a Latin philosophical expression, as is *negativa nihil* (the negation of nothingness), which actually ends up being an affirmation, the 'classic' double negative. *Norma normans* is another Latin expression which means the norm that norms, used nowadays most often to describe the nature of the authority of confessional church writings which are not themselves scripture but are seen to give a normative interpretation of scripture.

In the Gaelic alphabet Nion is number three and is represented by the Ash tree, which in George MacDonald's (1824-1905) classic *Phantastes* is an evil goblin. *Das Nichtige* is German for nothingness and was made common parlance in twentieth-century theology by Karl Barth. *Nihil obstat* used to be found stamped on the front of Catholic books approved for reading and simply meant that the local bishop or other church authority had no objection to the content. There was a time when good Catholics would not buy a book without a *nihil obstat* printed at the front. Now they are unlikely to buy a book if it does have one! And it seems that only through double negatives can N-words say something positive, and find no objection. And something extending to the Nth degree is without obvious end, unlimited – which is a nice double negating word with which to end our treatment of N.

Apart from A and I, O is the only letter that can stake claim to being a word in its own right. There is a great deal of divine symbolism connected with O, apart from its use in old hymns and psalms. O is omniscient, the One, and is an ancient symbol representing God as eternity as it has no beginning and no end.

O's place in the alphabet is vexed. In Greek the sound was represented both by Omega, the final letter of the Greek alphabet and symbol of the end of all things, and Omicron, which occurred in the middle of the alphabet. In the Latin alphabet omega fell away, and O's place was restricted to the middle of the alphabet, where it has remained. In appearance it looks like a monocled eye glass, which is ironic, as it is descended from Hebrew Ayin, which has its origins as a pictographic eye. 'Oscar's only ostrich oiled an orange owl' is from Seuss's *ABC*. I am certain he would have placed the action in Orrorroo, a phonetic palindrome and a town in South Australia, if only he had heard of it.

And O has a number of literary endorsements. The French humanist Geoffroy Tory (1480-1533) called it 'triumphant,' James Thurber (1894-1961) 'wonderful' and Edgar Alan Poe (1809-1849) a 'most sonorous vowel.' But most impressive of all is that Tolkien, after the Great War, spent an entire year working on the massive *Oxford English Dictionary* (*OED*), focused solely on the letter O!

P is the English version of the Greek letter Pi (π). It is silent in psalms and aspirated in phonetics. It provided us with our most famous tongue twister, the iambic 'Peter Piper picked a peck of pickled peppers' in which a peck is an old unit of measurement for the harvesting and selling of fruits and vegetables. It is much harder to say than 'puddle paddle battle,' which is form Seuss's *Fox in Socks* and is fought by beetles on a poodle.

P is a very literary letter with palindromes and poetry, not to mention all forms of paper, pulp, parchment and papyrus used in print. And a prose portal is the means by which one travels literally into literature in Jasper Fforde's *The Eyre Affair*. And my favourite P word would have to be pryzqxgl, which looks like someone fell onto their keyboard. It is actually from *The Magic of Oz* by L Frank Baum (1856-1919), which is the thirteenth and final book in the series. It is a magic word that a Munchkin named Bini Aru used to transform people and objects during his unsuccessful quest to conquer Oz. But it only works if pronounced correctly. Pity.

Q is a queer and quirky letter, with a tail, competing with K, which seems to have supplanted it in many cases, such as Koran instead of Qoran, kabbala instead of qabbala, and kibla instead of qibla. In fact, Ben Jonson (1572-1637) wanted to ditch the letter altogether in favour of K. In the Gaelic tree alphabet it is represented, appropriately, not only by the Apple but also by the Quince. And the reference to Q being unable to quit a word refers to its inability to ever be the last letter, always needing to be followed by usually unpronounced 'ue.' In fact, Q has great difficulty appearing anywhere without being followed by U. This, in turn, poses the question on which this poem ends. And for those interested, Quinella, apparently, is the name of the 'quick Queen of Quincy' from Seuss's *ABC*.

And why were we always told to mind our Ps and Qs? Apparently, according to one of the theories in the *OED*, it is because these were considered especially easy letters for children to confuse as they are both enclosed and come with a 'tail.' In fact, in most forms of print, the lower case versions look like mirror images of one another. So while it has come to mean 'behaving,' it was originally a bit of advice about spelling.

As a solo letter it is code for the gadgets man in James Bond films, and the powerful, troublesome being in *Star Trek the Next Generation*. It also pops up in abbreviated form in I.Q. (Intelligence Quotient) and BBQ (barbeque).

R is a tricky letter to pronounce. Many languages, like German, roll it, like a motorbike staring up. But in English, especially the US version, it is a flat sound that cannot even break into a mild growl. So R has a very different feel in different languages, and even among various English dialects. Few letters have had their personality so impacted by their sound as R. R is a racing, roaring sound with two long legs for running. Phoenician/Hebrew Resh (which symbolised movement) and Greek's one legged Rho stand behind it. Socrates (d. 399 BCE) saw the Greek Rho as the letter of motion, because of its sound. But Persius (34-62), the Latin poet, saw it as the *litera canina*, the canine letter, because it growls like a dog or wolf.

But R is more than action. It is also learning, with the three Rs of 'reading 'riting and 'rithmatic'. It is rhetoric and rhotics, rhythm and rhyme, and religion as well. It is runic Rad, which means 'riding' (Rad is, interestingly, the name for 'wheel' in German). So no matter how we look at it, Socrates seems to have been right. R has a very long pedigree as the letter of motion.

Here is a letter with issues. S is a sibilant, which means that it is a consonant that makes a hissing sound, with no hard stop. *Simul justus et peccator* is Latin, and means 'at the same time saint and sinner.' Luther used the phrase to describe the dual human nature. It seems to fit S well, too. From Hebrew we associate it with *Shabbat shalom* (Sabbath peace) and in Latin, *spiritus sanctus* (Holy Spirit). It is a letter associated with so many positive things. But we also get slithering serpentine words from S, with the sibilant naturally gravitating to describing all things slippery and snake-like.

S has its origins in the Hebrew letter Shin (ש), a pictogram of the sun, and ultimately was found in the proto-Sinaitic Phonecian alphabet, which was the *alphabeticus originalis*, the original or first alphabet.

In tongue twisters S comes second after only P's Peter Piper with 'Sally sold seashells by the seashore,' a phrase all children who have ever struggled with sibilants have come to fear, as much perhaps as *shibboleth*, the word the fleeing Ephraimite troops were forced to pronounce by the Gileadites (Judges 12:4-6) at the fords of the Jordan to prove their ethnic and linguistic origins. The word, ironically, means river or stream, and it was well-known the Ephraimites could not make the 'sh' sound.

And back to selling seashells by the seashore, the line originated in a song written by British songwriter Terry Sullivan in 1908: 'She sells sea-shells on the seashore./ The shells she sells are sea-shells, I'm sure./ For if she sells sea-shells on the sea-shore/ then I'm sure she sells sea-shore shells.' It was only natural that when adapted to a tongue-twister, the sea-shell seller would be named Sally.

S is also our sexy letter, asocial with seduction, succubus, scandal, shame and all things seedy. In fact, it is almost the scarlet S, which alludes to the scarlet A. And for those who are rusty on their Shakespeare, Justice Shallow is a character who appears in both *Henry IV* and *The Merry Wives of Windsor*. And sin without S, incidentally, is nothing more than the preposition 'in.'

Sans serif is French (or at the very least sans is, as the origin of serif, the little squiggly bits at the end of letters, is not clear) and it is a description of printed letters without decorative little swirls and tails.

T is the twentieth letter in our English alphabet, but in Hebrew and other early Semitic alphabets it occupied last place. Why it was shifted forward by the Greeks is not known, but it seemed destined to occupy an important place in all things theistic. A thane is a servant of a king, or in this case, of theos, or God. Thus T becomes in many ways a Thane of Theos. Plato (428-348 BCE) in *Phaedrus* tells the story of Theuth, the god of writing, who devised an alphabet. But it was rejected by the Egyptian king, Thamus, leaving that culture with their complex system of hieroglyphs, and the Phoenicians to develop the first known alphabet.

Joseph Campbell (1904-1987), in *Masks of God*, pointed out that Nordic followers of Thor, god of Thunder, long wore a 't' symbol to represent him. And T was also the symbol of the goddess Thalia, muse of poetry and comedic plays. But Greek Tau became much more famous as a symbol of the cross (literally a T) the tree of life and death associated with Christ, and thus the best-known and most widely recognised religious symbol of all time.

In modern text-messaging, U is the common form of you, and the truth of U takes on a double meaning. Historically, the Roman alphabet had no U, and V was used for both the consonantal and vowel sounds of the letter. To avoid confusion, English rounded the bottom of V to show when it was being used as a vowel. This change took place during the Renaissance period, but the use of V as U in English persisted into Elizabethan times, with the KJV and Shakespeare happy with forms such as 'vp' for 'up.' U also looks to children like an upside down umbrella.

Ulysses is the main character in Homer's *Odyssey*, and the reference to Ulysses in the poem points to the Greek letter upsilon. In the list of vowels U is always last, and the famous A-E-I-O-U gets a cameo in Goethe's (1749-1832) *Faust*, who has his demons chanting this refrain.

Sir Thomas More (1478-1535), with his friend Peter Giles (1486-1533), invented a language and alphabet for *Utopia*. Though not taken up by others, it was essentially the Roman alphabet, but with twenty-two instead of the twenty-three letters used in the Latin alphabet of their time. The images of all letters were based on geometric combinations of circles, triangles and squares. In an 1518 addendum to *Utopia*, Peter Giles wrote a small four line poem in Utopian. It is the only known original use of the constructed language and its alphabet.

As noted under Q, U is the ubiquitous companion of that letter. It is also a regular feature in prefixes, especially 'un' in English, but also under, uni and ultra. In German *über* is 'over' or 'super', and *ur* is 'ancient' or 'original'. Hence *übermenschlich* is 'superhuman', and *urgeschichtlich* is 'primeval'.

The reference to the vanquishing of V's vassal vowel refers to the double duty of both consonant and vowel served by V before the introduction of U. Victor Hugo (*Voyages and Expansions*) played on this by assigning the letters similar images, with U associated with the more rounded urn, and V with the more triangular vase. V is now free to express its own voice (*vox humana* = human voice). The confusion and remnants of this dual function still produces a vice versa (this way and that, or back to front) vacillation. The Vulgata is the name of the often maligned Latin translation of the Bible coming from St Jerome and used throughout the Middle Ages. It is literally a reference to the vulgar or common tongue of Jerome's day, which was Latin.

Victor V. Vulture is the name of the vaudeville ventriloquist from Graeme Base's *Animalia*, whose poster advertised that he would be 'vexatiously vocalizing.' *Voix celeste* is 'heavenly voice' and vespers, of course, is the traditional Western Christian service of evening prayer.

W is formed by the combination of two Vs, but oddly is known in English as a double U, partly owing the fact that U and V were once the same letter and many early forms of W, especially in lower case and cursive, were actually a double U in form. It is also interesting that in our alphabet W follows these two letters, which gave it life. The Greeks and Romans, as well as the Germans and others, had no such sound, and in the case the classical languages, no need for a letter to represent it. German has a W, but pronounce it as we would a V, showing again the links between these letters. The English use of W, it seems, owes something to the influence of the Celtic letter Wyn.

W in English became the questioning letter, with almost all basic questioning words such as who, where, what, why, when, whither and whence beginning with W. Walt Whitman (1819-1892) is a famous American poet of the late nineteenth century. And in Michigan, the state in the US in which I grew up, the state slogan which long graced every car number plate, was 'winter, water wonderland.' This was dropped some decades ago apparently because the concept of 'winter' without ski slopes was not beneficial for tourism. 'Wicked warrior WASPs' is from Graeme Base's *Animalia*. And WASPs, not used so much these days, stands for White Anglo-Saxon Protestants, who were exactly the kind of tourists Michigan once did not want to frighten off with the 'winter' tag. Wally is the character in the red and white striped shirt and hat that everyone seeks in the *Where's Wally* books, and *Wortschatz* is the German word for vocabulary.

Fewer words begin in English with X than any other letter of the alphabet. The reference to Graeme Base cheating with X in *Animalia* refers to his use of a mirror with the words 'Rex fox fix(ing) six sax(ophones)' to make it look like a phrase beginning with X words. One wonders why Wallace Stevens refers to it a 'vital, arrogant, fatal, dominant X' in his poem, 'The Motive for Metaphor.' While not useful for beginning words, it has done well as a symbol. Our English X looks the same as the Greek letter X (Chi, pronounced kai) which makes a sound like English K. Chi-rho is the name of the Christian symbol of a Greek Chi and rho (the first two letters in Christ) superimposed on one another to from a kind of cross.

X appears often in modern usage such as in X-box, x-ray, x-factor, x-rated, XXXX (which is a brand of Queensland beer that is either the best or worst beer in Australia, depending on whether or not one is from Queensland), X chromosome and X marks the spot. Not a lot of famous names begin with X, there are three famous people: Saint Francis Xavier, King Xerxes, and Xenophon, the author or the Australian politician. Of famous places there are two, and ironically one of them, Xanthus (an ancient city in Lycia, modern Turkey), no longer exists, and the other, Xanadu (from Samuel Taylor Coleridge's 1826 poem 'Kubla Kahn,') probably never did. Oh, and Xanthus was also the name of one of Achilles' two immortal horses in the Iliad. And only one deity is included, the Aztec Xipe, god of planting. And X equals ten in Roman numerals, making X letter number xxiv of our alphabet.

Y is a useful letter from Hebrew Yod and Greek Ypsilon, but appears on its own terms only in the late Roman alphabet. Yoda-speak refers to the unique sentence structure used by the famous *Star Wars* character by the same name. Y has been used to symbolise both philosophy and destiny and the letter was said, by the late Latin poet Maximinus, to have been invented by the philosopher Pythagoras (570-495 BCE). When Pythagoras invented the letter he is said to have portrayed it as a fork in the road, and illustrated it with a story of the young Hercules confronted with a choice between following a broad road, which a woman named Pleasure beckoned him to take, or a narrow road, toward which a woman called Virtue urged him.

In theology, the tetragrammaton (the four letters) refers to the four consonants of God's name, not to be pronounced, in the Old Testament, of which Y (Yod) was the first; יהוה (read from right to left). YHWH, or Yahweh, was corrupted into English 'Jehovah' removing Y from the picture altogether.

The Yeshiva yammer refers to the possibly Yiddish expression 'yadda, yadda, yadda,' common in North America and popularised by the *Seinfeld* show. It is used to say something like 'and so on and so forth.' And 'youthful yaks yodelling' is from Graeme Base's *Animalia*.

It is significant that Y was the first letter to inspire a poem, 'De Y littera' (The Letter Y) by Maximinus. Also, Alexander Pope (1688-1744) referred to Y as the Samian letter in his poem 'Dunciad'.

This is a reference to the Aegean island of Samos, birthplace of Pythagoras, whom legend says invented the letter. And Yanks is slang for Yankees, a pejorative name given to Americans by British soldiers at the time of the war of revolution, or independence, depending on one's perspective. After the early victories of the colonists at Lexington and Concord in 1775, they adopted the word as a badge of honour.

Z, which finds its way firmly at the end of our alphabet, has replaced Omega for representing the 'end,' and we now speak of A-Z. Z is everywhere pronounced Zed, except in America, where it is Zee. It is the only letter in the English alphabet, therefore, with two names. Other names it has held include Izzard, Uzard, Ezrod, Zard and Zad! It is from Quenton Tarantino's American film *Pulp Fiction* that we get the phrase 'Zed is dead.'

The 'pseudonymous' dig at Shakespeare is reference to the many theories that the plays may have been written by another. And 'Thou whoreson Zed. Thou unnecessary letter' is from *King Lear*. Zeta and Zayin are, respectively, the Greek and Hebrew forebears of Z. Z, which the Latins picked up from the Etruscans to represent the Greek sound Zeta, gradually fell into disuse and was even officially stricken for a time from the Latin alphabet by a zealous official named Appius Claudius Caecus in or about 312.

When it made its reappearance there was really nowhere to put it but at the end of the alphabet with the other newcomer, Y.

A ziggurat is an ancient pyramidal style building from Mesopotamia. A zeugma is a word, usually an adjective, made to apply to two very different words in a sentence, as in the example of zesty being applied to both Zed and zeppelins. And zymotic refers to a contagion that develops after an infection.

This long alphabet poem, with the last line of each stanza tying in verbally with the first line of the next stanza, finishes appropriately with the last line of the poem repeating the first line exactly, the only verbatim link in the twenty-six stanzas.

also published by **immortalise**

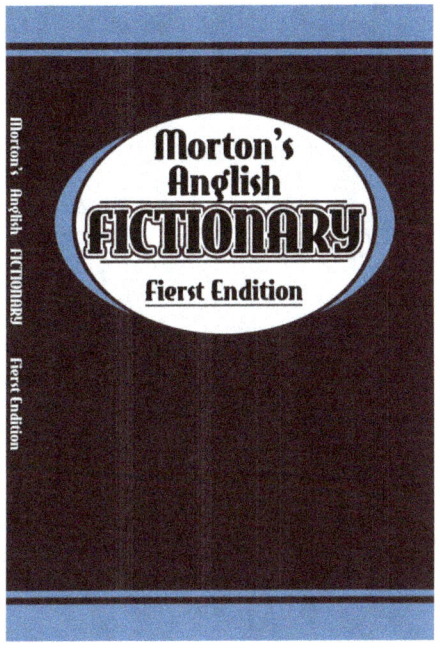

This is the Fierst Endition of Morton Benning's painstakingly alphabetised and sporadically proofread catalogue of fabricated neologisms featuring somewhat humorous daffynitions and phonetic pronunciation guides. We hope you'll enjoy it, or at least laugh politely and tell people you did, because that's good for sales.

also published by **immortalise**

A humorous look at life through the eyes of a young geeky guy with a unique sense of humour. Tragically, Cedric did not survive his battle with mental illness to see his art work in print, but his friends and family have collected it and presented it in finished form so that it may be enjoyed by all.

www.ingramcontent.com/pod-product-compliance
Lightning Source LLC
Chambersburg PA
CBHW070437010526
44118CB00014B/2089